KEVIN WILLIAMSON founde
Rebel Inc Magazine (1992–1
ing Editor at Canongate Book
imprint.

In 1997 he wrote the infl
Party Line, a political polemic ....y. He won the
2005 *Robert Louis Stevenson Award* and in 2007 his debut
poetry collection *In A Room Darkened* was published by Two
Ravens Press. That same year he co-founded *Bella Caledonia*,
widely recognised as one of the most influential Scottish current
affairs websites.

In 2011 he co-founded *Neu! Reekie!* – a cross-arts cabaret –
and in the summer of 2011 he wrote and starred in the successful
Edinburgh Festival Fringe show *Robert Burns: Not In My Name*.

He lives with his family in Leith.

ASIF, CRAIG, CRAIG, DAVID, KEVIN, GEORGE, PAUL, STEPHEN AND
VICTOR were all inmates at Kilmarnock Prison during 2012 and
2013. Some are still serving sentences. Others are now free.

INDEPENDENT MINDS

New poetry from HMP Kilmarnock

Edited by Kevin Williamson

Luath Press Limited
EDINBURGH
www.luath.co.uk

First published 2013

ISBN: 978-1-908373-96-0

The paper used in this book is recyclable. It is made from
low chlorine pulps produced in a low energy, low emissions manner
from renewable forests.

The publishers acknowledge the support of

ALBA | CHRUTHACHAIL

towards the publication of this volume.

Printed and bound by
Bell & Bain Ltd., Glasgow

Typeset in 10.5 point Sabon

Images © the National Trust for Scotland unless otherwise stated.

To free minds.

Contents

Acknowledgements

Special thanks to all those who helped make this book happen:

Craig Maxwell, Cara Garven, Hannah Teasdale, Nat Edwards, Esther Rutter, James King, Gavin MacDougall, the Robert Burns Birthplace Museum, and especially the prisoners and staff at HMP Kilmarnock.

If I'm design'd yon lordling's slave
By Nature's law design'd
Why was an independent wish
E'er planted in my mind?

ROBERT BURNS

Foreword

INDEPENDENT MINDS

... even if you found yourself in some prison, whose walls let in none of the world's sound – wouldn't you still have your childhood, that jewel beyond all price, that treasure house of memories? Turn your attention to it. Try to raise up the sunken feelings of this enormous past; your personality will grow stronger, your solitude will expand and become a place where you can live in the twilight, where the noise of other people passes by, far in the distance.

Rainer Maria Rilke, Letters To A Young Poet

WHEN I WAS OFFERED the chance to work with a group of prisoners in HMP Kilmarnock on a Robert Burns related project, I jumped at it. I love the poetry of Robert Burns. I read it to my children and I perform it in public. There's a magic to Burns that transcends age, class, gender and nationality. I don't need much encouragement to share my passion for this wonderful writer.

When Jeremy Paxman famously dismissed Burns as little more than a writer of 'sentimental doggerel' it said more about the TV presenter than the poet. Burns's poetry is not only wide-ranging and complex, and written with great technical virtuosity, it has a vitality, importance and social relevance very few poets will ever achieve.

It's not just his writing. Like many Scots, I'm fascinated by the man. Burns was a complicated character, it has to be said, and someone who lived an incredible life in tumultuous times. His premature death at the age of just 37 may have robbed Scotland of its authentic national Bard but his reputation grows with each passing year.

Robert Burns has become so entwined with the history and culture of the country that produced him that even now, 250 years after his birth, if we put our ear to the ground, we can still feel the reverberations of his life. As Scotland approaches its own witching hour, or what has been described as our date with destiny, the shadow of Burns looms large.

Consider events that took place 400 miles apart on 25

January 2012. The UK Parliament in London and the Scottish Parliament in Edinburgh were both in session and both discussed the forthcoming referendum on Scottish Independence. Eleanor Laing, a backbench Conservative MP, set the hares running when she stood up in Westminster and said:

'Today is the anniversary of the great Scottish poet Robert Burns. Does the Prime Minster agree with Burns's impassioned plea for the unity of our nation when he says in his poem *The Dumfries Volunteers*:

Be Britain still to Britain true
Among ourselves united
For never but by British hands
May British wrongs be righted.'

David Cameron, the British Prime Minister, added:

The point she makes is a good one. And Burns Night will be celebrated not just across Scotland but across the whole of the United Kingdom and indeed in many parts of the world. And when I hear the Scottish Nationalists, who are so keen to leave the United Kingdom, yet so anxious to have a referendum, they should remember Burns's words when he referred to the 'wee cowering sleekit cowering timorous beastie, oh what a panic's in thy breastie'.

The Scottish First Minister, Alex Salmond, responded:

I'm told there are members of the House of Lords who believe that it is in their province to set boundaries on what Scotland can and cannot do. Perhaps they should be reminded that Burns's great hymn to equality has been heard in this Parliament before.

Alex Salmond was referring to the famous occasion when Sheena Wellington put goosebumps down the spines of an entire nation as she sang Burns's great egalitarian anthem *A Man's A Man* at the opening of the Scottish Parliament in 1999.

This was mostly good-natured political banter. But what was less remarked upon was the truly unique significance of this political exchange. Robert Burns, a farm labourer from Ayrshire, had been dead for over two centuries yet to mark his birthday, in two separate Parliaments, his reputation for plain speaking and political integrity was invoked by two governments to bolster their diametrically opposite political views. When you consider this from the poet's perspective – any poet's perspective – this is quite staggering. Robert Burns is clearly much more than just another poet, but someone whose poetry and politics still matter, and still carry some clout.

I was thinking about this when I began planning a series of poetry workshops with the prisoners at HMP Kilmarnock. I wanted to go beyond the lazy clichés and shortbread tin mythology that surround Burns and explore the lesser-known side of Robert Burns the political radical.

The project, set up by the Robert Burns Birthplace Museum, was called *Independent Minds* and sought to explore whether it was, as Burns claimed, a curse to be an independent thinker. Burns was no stranger to trouble and more recent biographers such as Robert Crawford have speculated that the British government considered him a dangerous subversive. In his last few years spent in Dumfries the threat of arrest, imprisonment or even deportation may have been a reality. There was a fair chance some of the prisoners might relate to this aspect of the Burns story.

I also felt it would be interesting to discuss some of the contradictions highlighted in the parliamentary exchange described above, because, let's face it, David Cameron and Alex Salmond can't both be right. (Or could they?) I was also keen to find out if the prisoners would respond to Burns in their own words.

I doubt if there is any poet better placed than Robert Burns to build such a project around. His appeal is universal and he remains peerless in his claim to be a national bard. For some he is the poet of wild, untamed nature. For others, Bob Dylan included, he was the love poet extraordinaire. Women say they adore him for his tender romantic side yet he's also perceived as a man's man, a tough labourer who worked hard and played hard, who liked the lasses and enjoyed a guid drink. He is considered a champion of the common people. Even among those who might normally run a mile from poetry nobody is embarrassed to say they like Robert Burns.

Each workshop was structured around a different subject such as Burns's Place Among Scottish Literature, Burns & The Scottish

Language, Burns & Independence, Burns & War, or Burns & Slavery. The educational facilities in HMP Kilmarnock are pretty decent and we were able to screen short films and extracts from TV programmes to help illustrate the subject and get a discussion going. One thing you quickly learn when you organise political discussions in a prison is that the guys aren't short of opinions. And that's putting it mildly. I had to compete to get my tuppence worth in as much as anyone else, which is the way it should be.

Inevitably, in a project called *Independent Minds*, we discussed Scottish Independence and some of the guys' thoughts on that subject can be read in this book. For my part, from spending time with these guys, I've come to the conclusion that it's a disgrace that prisoners are not being allowed to vote in Scotland's Independence Referendum in 2014. Not only will the outcome affect them for the rest of their lives but the very act of voting is about engaging with civic society and feeling part of it. Surely, as a society, we should want all incarcerated prisoners to take steps down that road. Is that not part of the rehabilitation process?

In one workshop we watched a film on the realities of slavery. In the 18th century Jamaica was the jewel in the crown of the British empire. It produced more wealth for the Empire than any other colony. Yet all of the riches derived from Jamaica came from brutal chattel slavery which involved the systematic abuse, exploitation, rape, torture and murder of black Africans. Inevitably this meant addressing another question: Why did a poet who championed equality even consider emigrating to Jamaica?

With the Robert Burns Birthplace Museum not far along the road from HMP Kilmarnock, artefacts related to Robert Burns, and relevant to the workshops, were brought into the prison. On this occasion a set of wooden manacles worn by African slaves was taken into the class. All the guys tried them on. Although a few jokes were cracked at the time, such is prison life, knowing who had worn them all those years ago had an effect.

The writing came in the second part of each workshop once ideas and emotions were flowing. Writing tutors approach workshops in different ways. I prefer to begin with metre, rhyme and form rather than free verse. Some of Burns's most famous poems – such as 'To A Mouse' and 'Address To A Haggis' – are written in a uniquely Scottish verse called a 'Standard Habbie' which dates back to the late 17th century. The 'Standard Habbie' has six lines in each verse where the first three lines and the fifth have eight syllables and rhyme with each other. Likewise the fourth and sixth line have four syllables and also rhyme. The guys soon picked it up and produced some great work written in Standard Habbie verse, some of which are featured in this anthology.

I'll admit I was a wee bit nervous about going into the jail to take poetry workshops, because it was outside my comfort zone, but they were a great bunch of guys. I learned a lot from listening to them and enjoyed their craic. Literacy among the prison population is very low and may be a big part of the reason why so many good people end up in jail. We need more projects which encourage literacy among prisoners or help tap into their creativity. It's win-win for everyone.

The quality of the finished work is contained within these pages and speaks for itself. Some of the guys had never written poetry before and it took sustained concentration and effort just to get the lines down on paper. I'm very proud of what every single one of the guys achieved in such a short time.

Hope you enjoy the poetry too.

Kevin Williamson
2013

Lines Written On A Bank Of Scotland One Guinea Note

Wae worth thy pow'r, thou cursed leaf!
Fell source of all my woe and grief!
For lake o' thee I've lost my lass;
For lake o' thee I scrimp my glass;
I see the children of Affliction
Unaided, thro thy curst restriction,
I've seen th' Oppressor's cruel smile,
Amid his hapless victims spoil;
And for thy potence vainly wished,
To crush the Villain in the dust:
For lake o' thee I leave this much-lov'd shore,
Never perhaps to greet old Scotland more!

ROBERT BURNS

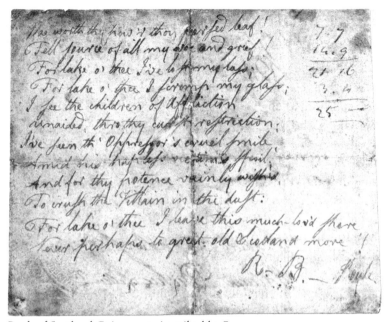

Bank of Scotland Guinea note inscribed by Burns
Robert Burns Birthplace Museum 3.6106

INDEPENDENT MINDS

Slavery

Was I a slave in my past life?
Or has he caught me up in this life?
So how come it seems to work for you
But not for me. Open your eyes
Cos it is time for them to see.
It's not the 1850s now.
We are not your captured slaves.
The days are gone. History ended.
Colour should not be an issue.
It's not political or historical.
My blood, your blood, it's just the same.
Anger. Justice. Colour.

ASIF

War

Artillery target ready.
Detonation waiting steady.
Shouting walkie-talkie crackles.
I'm the scumbag in shackles.
What did I get myself in?

ASIF

To My Mum

Dear Mum you are my only one
'A' class, you are second to none.
These lines come from your loving son.
      I miss you, Mum.
When this is all over and done
      We'll have some fun.

ASIF

Such A Parcel Of Rogues In A Nation

Farewell to a' our Scottish fame,
  Fare weel our ancient glory;
Fareweel even to the Scottish name,
  Sae fam'd in martial story.
Now Sark rins o'er the Solway sands,
  And Tweed rins to the ocean,
To mark where Englands province stands,
  Such a parcel of rogues in a nation.

What force or guile could not subdue,
  Thro' many warlike ages,
Is wrought now by a coward few,
  For hireling traitors wages.
The English steel we could disdain,
  Secure in valour's station;
But English gold has been our bane,
  Such a parcel of rogues in a nation.

O would, or I had seen the day
  That treason thus could sell us,
My auld grey head had lien in clay
  Wi' Bruce and loyal Wallace!
But pith & power, till my last hour,
  I'll mak this declaration;
We're bought & sold for English gold
  Such a parcel of rogues in a nation!

ROBERT BURNS

Such a parcel of rogues in a nation— A Song—

Fareweel to a' our Scotish fame,
  Fareweel our ancient glory;
Fareweel even to the Scotish name,
  Sae fam'd in martial story!
Now Sark rins o'er the Solway-sands,
  And Tweed rins to the ocean,
To mark where England's province stands—
  Such a parcel of rogues in a nation.

What guile or force could not subdue,
  Thro' many warlike ages,
Is wrought now by a coward few
  For hireling traitor's wages:
The English steel we could disdain,
  Secure in valour's station;
But English gold has been our bane,
  Such a parcel of rogues in a nation.

O would, ere I had seen the day
  That Treason thus could sell us,
My auld gray head had lien in 'clay,
  Wi' Bruce & loyal Wallace!

Manuscript, 'Such a Parcel of Rogues in a Nation'
Robert Burns Birthplace Museum 3.6186

Drugs

I've taken drugs, I love the stuff
cocaine, heroin, lots of puff.
I love getting high, right oot my nut.
Don't tell my Mum, she'd kick my butt.

I took my first drug at fifteen.
It was vals and a bit of green.
Soon after that I had some E.
Next was some speed then LSD.

Vals were sublime and green was good.
Speed, acid, E lifted my mood.
I took so much then took some more,
I was greedy, trouble in store...

So I moved onto some cocaine.
Took far too much, I went insane.
I tanned a quarter in one night,
then went to Tesco – what a sight!

That's when I really went to town
and couldn't resist golden brown,
then things didn't go very well,
I was under the Devil's spell.

So all was good but just don't toot,
yes be morally dissolute!
Illicit substances, good times.
Just don't fund it with silly crimes.

CRAIG

Independence

Referendum a year away
will we fair Scots have our day,
when we can shout and sing out loud
This is Scotland! No English allowed.

For centuries oor wee nation
told oor place by the occupation.
Kept at bay and always put down,
ruled by 'Eng-ur-lund' and her crown.

A land of fighters some might say.
Yes, we chased the Romans away!
A land of inventors oor folks,
Irn-Bru, telly and knitted soaks!

We're rich in culture it's a fact.
Humour, booze and plenty of tact.
Robert Burns, Stein and Connelly
Poetry, football, comedy.

The States to Japan love oor style.
You'll see us on Jeremy Kyle!
'Men in kilts?! It's a skirt!!' they joke.
Think they jocks had too much tae toke!

Every New Year there is a song
sung in Australia and Hong Kong.
It's Auld Lang Syne by Robert Burns.
Now sing along, we'll all take turns.

Tell your friends we need to promote
that in one year we're off to vote.
If you vote Yes we'll have our day
then shout Freedom with dignity.

CRAIG

To A Nuclear Weapon

Silent, waiting tae blow yer top.
Button pressed and you'll be dropped.
You'll kill and maim and all for what?
      You have no choice.
Unlike humans you can't be taught,
      So let's rejoice.

CRAIG

Me

I'm from a place called Irvine town.
It ain't that nice. It makes me frown.
Je m'appelle Craig, vingt-sept ans.
J'habite a Irvine en Ecosse.

Now I'm not French don't get me wrong
I know some words, couldn't sing a song,
learned it at school, should a' stuck in
but I preferred weed and straight gin.

I love music and politics
but British MPs make me sick!
Foreign policy, what a shame.
Bomb the Arabs and take no blame.

The jobs I've had are quite barmy,
sales, cleaning and the army,
but now I sit quite thin and pale
in Bowhouse prison, I'm in the jail!

In here you're labelled 'you're all thugs!'
Listen to mum, 'Stay off the drugs!'
I'll serve my time. I'll stay in line.
When I'm out, I'll buy tonic wine.

But as I sit writing these words,
all I think of is drugs and burds.
In jail I sit, but when I'm done
I'll knuckle down for my wee son.

CRAIG

Slavery

What do you think of slavery?
Hardship, torture and misery.
Black folks used in a shameful way,
by the upper echelons of society.

People say it's in the past,
'Yeah slavery's cruel. It didn't last!'
But have a look around today.
Slavery hasn't gone away.

It takes many different forms.
People abused and treated like worms.
The one per cent, the people on top,
people that work in a Chinese sweatshop.

Controlled and used from an ivory tower.
Rockefellers and Rothschilds have all the power.
Will we ever be free again?
We never were, goodbye, Amen.

CRAIG

To A Kerb Crawler

You come out when it's dark, at night,
Scantily clad, oh, what a sight.
Your looks would make the punters fight,
      A lonely lass,
Bairn left at home. This can't be right,
      A life so crass.

CRAIG

On A Scotch Bard Gone To The West Indies

A' ye wha live by sowps o' drink,
A' ye wha live by crambo-clink,
A' ye wha live and never think,
    Come, mourn wi' me!
Our *billie's* gien us a' a jink,
    An' owre the Sea.

Lament him a' ye rantan core,
Wha dearly like a random-splore;
Nae mair he'll join the *merry roar*,
    In social key;
For now he's taen anither shore,
    An' owre the Sea!

The bonie lasses weel may wiss him,
And in their dear *petitions* place him:
The widows, wives, an' a' may bless him,
    Wi' tearfu' e'e;
For weel I wat they'll sairly miss him
    That's owre the Sea!

O Fortune, they hae room to grumble!
Hadst thou taen aff some drowsy bummle,
Wha can do nought but fyke an' fumble,
    'Twad been nae plea;
But he was gleg as onie wumble,
    That's owre the Sea!

Auld, cantie KYLE may weepers wear,
An' stain them wi' the saut, saut tear:
'Twill mak her poor, auld heart, I fear,
    In flinders flee:
He was her *Laureat* monie a year,
    That's owre the Sea!

He saw Misfortune's cauld *Nor-west*
Lang-mustering up a bitter blast;
A Jillet brak his heart at last,
    Ill may she be!
So, took a birth afore the mast,
    An' owre the Sea.

To tremble under Fortune's cummock,
On a scarce a bellyfu' o' *drummock*,
Wi' his proud, independant stomach,
    Could ill agree;
So, row't his hurdies in a *hammock*,
    An' owre the Sea.

He ne'er was gien to great misguidin,
Yet coin his pouches wad na bide in;
Wi' him it ne'er was *under hidin*;
    He dealt it free:
The *Muse* was a' that he took pride in,
    That's owre the Sea.

Jamaica bodies, use him weel,
An' hap him in a cozie biel:
Ye'll find him ay a dainty chiel,
    An' fou o' glee:
He wad na wrang'd the vera *Deil*,
    That's owre the Sea.

Farewell, my *rhyme-composing billie*!
Your native soil was right ill-willie;
But may ye flourish like a lily,
    Now bonilie!
I'll toast ye in my hindmost *gillie*,
    Tho' owre the Sea!

ROBERT BURNS

Detail from *The Jolly Beggars* engraved by Alexander Green
Robert Burns Birthplace Museum 3.8174

4 Haikus

Raindrops falling down.
They run, heading for cover.
Troubled minds forget.

Music is joy and
Sorrow does not belong here,
But loss is heavy.

Fond memories last,
In times of need uplifting,
Relieving sadness.

Anger from within
Controlling my emotions
Rage bursting outward.

CRAIG

A Certain Kind Of Slavery

Feeling like a slave to my schizophrenic illness
People don't really understand this illness is suffocating.
The delusions I believe are: Are they fake? Real?
Are the voices that are bombarding me
Some other beings communicating?
Am I just crazy? To me it's all hazy.
The doctors and nurses watching my every move.
The pills they give a controlling kind of suffocation.
The doctors listen eagerly, the nurses always observing,
Dissecting my life so far, trying to understand.
They say they can help.
It all seems to me like an unnecessary suffocation.
Even when I'm in my home, I'm watching the clock, waiting
For time to take my pills.
Yes, I'm a slave to my ever-increasing medication.
To me it's all a certain kind of slavery.

CRAIG

The Slave's Lament

It was in sweet Senegal that my foes did me enthrall
For the lands of Virginia-ginia O;
Torn from that lovely shore, and must never see it more,
And alas! I am weary, weary O!
Torn from that lovely shore, and must never see it more;
And alas! I am weary, weary O!

All on that charming coast is no bitter snow and frost,
Like the lands of Virginia-ginia O:
There streams for ever flow, and there flowers for ever blow,
And alas! I am weary, weary O!
There streams for ever flow, and there flowers for ever blow,
And alas! I am weary, weary O!

The burden I must bear, while the cruel scourge I fear,
In the lands of Virginia-ginia O;
And I think on friends most dear, with the bitter, bitter tear,
And alas! I am weary, weary O!
And I think on friends most dear, with the bitter, bitter tear,
And alas! I am weary, weary O!

ROBERT BURNS

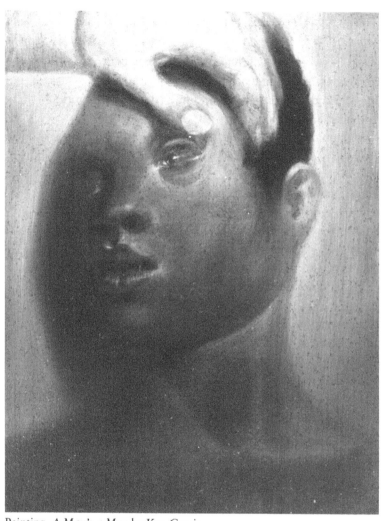

Painting, *A Man's a Man* by Ken Currie
Robert Burns Birthplace Museum (private loan)

Forgive And Forget

Can we now forgive humanity
For all its abuse and brutality?
Wars in the east; wars in the west
For politicians, 'cause they know best.

It's in our interests or so they say
Those power games they make us play.
Fight and kill in the Lord God's name.
So who is guilty and who's to blame?

Be it opium, gold, diamonds or oil
There's been so much blood soaked into the soil
And brainwashed minds now rotten to the core,
So how can mankind take much more?

It's time to forgive, but do we forget
Or forever live in the shadow of threat?
So Mother, Father, Sister and Brother
Live now in peace and love one another.

DAVID

To The Drink

Escape towards the social brink
To take away the joy to think
Amid the womb of lily the pink
       Wine, women and song.
Raise a glass to the demon drink,
       So right, it's wrong.

A cairy-oot for a cairy-on
No care or want where you belong
A party piece for a sing-along
       Whisky and beer.
for themes or schemes where we came from
       Near, dear and queer.

DAVID

Lions Or Sheep

In aw the nooks and cracks of faces
In aw the toons and social places
In some who sleep and in some who weep
Those lions have now turned into sheep
Where social cracks divide and rule
And anglify our weans in school.
Do as they say. Don't do as they do.
Don't be like them, just be like you.
William Wallace was so brave
But now he's turning in his grave
Stripped to the bone, ignore the pain.
Old Scotia, rise and be a nation again.
Through wind and tide those powers reside
With taxes taken, we people provide.
Their twisted tongues make lies seem true,
So do what they say. Don't do as they do.
These rogues who rule upon this nation
Try to poison the next generation.
Stand firm and free our thoughts to think.
Don't let them wash you down the sink.
So, independent minds, now see!
Break away! Stand firm! Be free!
It's all for one and one for all
And await the lion rampant's call.

DAVID

Sail Away

Slaves of men subdued in pain
Amid a ship to go insane
Each man's fight for his own survival
As masters await on their arrival
Torn away from their father's land
Where footsteps left upon the sand
Condemnation of a nation
Pain and hunger, violation
Blood beat and dread
Heave and haul until they're dead
Jump off the ship and liberate
Cos slavery is not your fate
Until the colour of a man's skin
Has no more significance
Than the colour of his eyes
Until that day
The dream of lasting peace
World citizenship
Rule of international morality
Can be pursued yet never attained.

DAVID

Bruce To His Troops On The Eve Of The Battle Of Bannockburn

Scots, wha hae wi' WALLACE bled,
Scots, wham BRUCE has aften led,
Welcome to your gory bed,
    Or to victorie!

Now's the day, and now's the hour;
See the front o' battle lour;
See approach proud Edward's power –
    Chains and slaverie!

Wha will be a traitor-knave?
Wha can fill a coward's grave?
Wha sae base as be a slave?
    Let him turn and flee!

Wha, for SCOTLAND's king and law,
Freedom's sword will strongly draw,
FREE-MAN stand, or FREE-MAN fa',
    Let him follow me!

By oppression's woes and pains!
By your sons in servile chains!
We will drain our dearest veins,
    But they shall be free!

Lay the proud usurpers low!
Tyrants fall in every foe!
LIBERTY's in every blow!
    Let us DO, or DIE!!!

ROBERT BURNS

Bannockburn — tune, Lewie Gordon —
Bruce to his troops —

Scots, wha hae wi' Wallace bled;
Scots, wham Bruce has often led;
Welcome to your gory bed,
    Or to glorious victorie.

Now's the day, & now's the hour;
See the front of battle lour;
See approach, proud Edward's power,
    Edward! Chains & slaverie!

Wha will be a traitor knave?
Wha can fill a coward's grave?
Wha sae base as be a slave?
    Traitor! Coward! turn & flie!

Wha for Scotland's king & law
Freedom's sword will strongly draw,
Free-man stand, or Free-man fa',
    Caledonian, on wi' me!

By Oppression's woes & pains!
By your sons in servile chains!

Manuscript, *Bruce to his troops*
Robert Burns Birthplace Museum 3.6203

Money Power Desire

Standing here with my whip and chains
Just bought my slaves they'll feel my pain
Just off the boat I took them home
They look so lost so much alone
We'll take the men and take the wives
But not the kids who can't provide
Kids left at home all left behind
Not one penny dread in their minds
I was there when I was young
My family poor now I stand with gun
Power it can go to your head
The way I was I do instead
My wife and kids tucked in their beds
They don't know my childhood dread
My fortune made I'll soon retire
But Slavery = Money Power Desire.

KEVIN

To A Mouse

On turning her up in her Nest, with the Plough,
November, 1785

Wee, sleeket, cowran, tim'rous *beastie*,
O, what a panic's in thy breastie!
Thou need na start awa sae hasty,
   Wi' bickering brattle!
I wad be laith to rin an' chase thee,
   Wi' murd'ring *pattle*!

I'm truly sorry Man's dominion,
Has broken Nature's social union,
An' justifies that ill opinion,
   Which makes thee startle
At me, thy poor, earth-born companion,
   An' *fellow-mortal*!

I doubt na, whyles, but thou may *thieve*;
What then? poor beastie, thou maun live!
A *daimen-icker* in a *thrave*
   'S a sma' request;
I'll get a blessin wi' the lave,
   An' never miss't!

Thy wee bit *housie*, too, in ruin!
It's silly wa's the win's are strewin!
An' naething, now, to big a new ane,
   O' foggage green!
An' bleak *December's winds* ensuin,
   Baith snell an' keen!

Thou saw the fields laid bare an' waste,
An' weary Winter comin fast,
An' cozie here, beneath the blast,
    Thou thought to dwell,
Till crash! the cruel *coulter* past
    Out thro' thy cell.

That wee bit heap o' leaves an' stibble,
Has cost thee monie a weary nibble!
Now thou's turn'd out, for a' thy trouble,
    But house or hald,
To thole the winter's *sleety dribble*,
    An' *cranreuch* cauld!

But, Mousie, thou art no thy-lane,
In proving *foresight* may be vain:
The best laid schemes o' Mice an 'Men
    Gang aft agley,
An' lea'e us nought but grief an' pain,
    For promis'd joy!

Still thou art blest, compar'd wi' *me*!
The *present* only toucheth thee:
But, Och! I *backward* cast my e'e.
    On prospects drear!
An' *forward*, tho' I canna *see*,
    I *guess* an' *fear*!

ROBERT BURNS

Engraving by John Le Conte after a painting by Gourlay Steell,
Burns turning up a mouse with his plough
Robert Burns Birthplace Museum 3.8103

INDEPENDENT MINDS

On A Guid Scotch Bard Ill-Advisedly Gone To The West Indies

Aw ye wha dwell in foreign lands
Aw ye wha live by second hand
Aw ye wha idle wi the grand
      Now feel for me!
This billie's sunk in sinking sands
      Across the sea.

I curse the cruel heavin' waves
The murderous turn o' brutal lathes
Pit Senegal Man in early graves
      His Beauty tae.
The airns and horsewhip sugar craves
      A bluidy spray.

I didna ken Auld Cloots wis here
In ev'ry sweetn'd planters ear
Young stamped banes cry oot Despair!
      See naught beyond.
While wretched o' the Earth compare
      Their Guinea's bond.

Jamaica bodies used them weel
An tore them oot frae cozie biels
Paid coin at Mercat for the chiels
      Scored their prize.
They widda kissed the vera De'il
      Wha made them wise.

Fareweel, this bardie's seen enough
His native soil wis nae sae tough
But here it shakes wi Satan's laugh
      O let me hame!
A foolish plan has come tae naught
      I cry wi shame.

KEVIN WILLIAMSON

Sonnet for Gaza

Shalom! This is not a time for clandestine poets
To hurl shoes over Jericho's fortified walls.
Stay calm. The stench of exploding verse
Will not deter the invading tanks of Saul.

You bragged that the lost tribe of Israel
Would not be dragged through the eye of a needle.
There would be corrective fury. An iron heel.
An eye for an eyelash. A fire that is truly biblical.

So you came in Numbers. The Genesis of hate.
Judges & Kings till the Job was complete.
Holy revenge against David's puny catapult.
Daniel dismembered by the lion's savage maul.

When you heard the words 'suffer little children'
Did you think it was one of the Ten Commandments?

KEVIN WILLIAMSON

Thanksgiving For A Naval Victory

Ye hypocrites! are these your pranks?
To murder men and give God thanks!
Desist, for shame!-proceed no further;
God won't accept your thanks for Murther!

ROBERT BURNS

Detail from *The Soldier's Return* engraved by John Faed
Robert Burns Birthplace Museum 3.2535

A Glasgow Childhood

Ower the greeny, kids frae the scheme
Pirates, cowboys, all kinds of dreams.
Be what you want till darkness falls,
Heading home back ower the walls.
Dreams forgotten lie on the ground.
But picked up once more when
The morn comes around.

School on Monday. Whit a bore!
Struggle up. Whit a chore!
Maw shouting, 'Move it! Get oot that door!'
Cannae wait to get home and ower that wa'
To the greeny once more to play football.
Pick up our dreams that we left behind.
Be Cowboys and Indians in our greeny-filled minds.

Trip to the toon on yon dirty bus,
Smell o' diesel hangs ower us.
Fag ends on floor, beer cans too.
Bus is honking, air is too.

Choking in the fug of smokers' hell,
Leavin' the bus fresh air in lungs.
Damn these shopping days, damn them to hell.

Bus to Largs, waiting in a queue,
On to Millport with the ferry crew,
Seagulls screaming up in the sky,
Standin' back from the edge, fear in the eye
O' a child's awed face
On the Millport ferry, for the Summer race.

Big stane fish high up on the beach
Hunners o' weans just couldnae reach
That big pented fish up yon beach.
Glaikit faces you couldnae teach.
A day oot doon the watter
Wis aw that they wanted.
Snottery nose, greetin'-faced weans chips in hand
Ice-cream smiles to see the big rock
In the Millport sand.

Awa' back hame on the tea train
Wait tae next year to dae it aw again.
Bags of rocks, buckets of sand
Come frae the rock pented in the sand.

GEORGE

Cargo

A price to be paid for their misery.
The price was high but life was cheap.
The dead they cast in waters deep.
In the dark hold they lay shivering and cold.
They were hungry. Disease was rife.
At what cost a slave's life?

The white man stood tall and strong,
Listening to the negro song,
But they didn't care. They pitied them not.
On and on the ship did sail.
The negroes frightened in their floating jail.

They were beaten, chained, starved to death.
No freedom for them on this earth.
The auctioneers cruel, cruel men
Laid into them again and again.

Herded like cattle to a life
They didn't know.
Starved and beaten.
Frightened and scared.
They cowered together in the decks below.

Branded and starved.
Beaten and weak.
Those poor creatures could not stand on their feet.

GEORGE

War

Amidst destruction, chaos, death
My target below lit the night
Faster and faster downward they fall
Taking lives in a fiery ball.

Bullets and blood hand in hand
Wars fought in foreign lands
Lives taken, cheap at the cost
price of bullets more lives lost.

GEORGE

I Murder Hate

I murder hate by field or flood,
　Tho' glory's name may screen us;
In wars at home I'll spend my blood,
　Life-giving wars of Venus.
The deities that I adore,
　Are social Peace and Plenty;
I'm better pleas'd to make one more
　Than be the death of twenty.

I would not die like Socrates,
　For all the fuss of Plato;
Nor would I with Leonidas,
　Nor yet would I with Cato:
The zealots of the Church and State
　Shall ne'er my mortal foes be;
But let me have bold Zimri's fate,
　Within the arms of Cozbi!

ROBERT BURNS

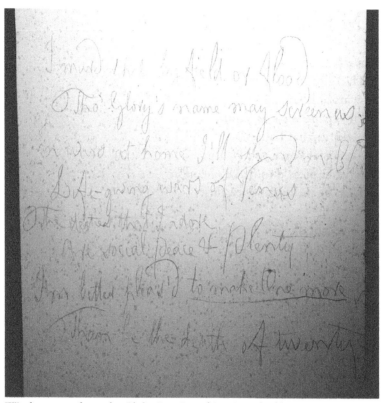

Window pane from the Globe Inn, Dumfries, inscribed by Burns
Robert Burns Birthplace Museum 3.4003

Prisoner Against Reliance

Drive us to court and bring us back.
We have enough on mind without being attacked.
Your position gives you no right.
Your verbal abuse to get me to bite!

PAUL

The Con Wi' Keys

Remand wing, ye've stied fur nine moon.
Woppers bein shipped, Lowmoss soon.
Information fur liberation.
        I'm hidin noo.
Mind whit side o' the fence ye roan.
        Naughty but true.

PAUL

To Cameron And Clegg

Yis sit doon there, Westminster,
Plottin 'n' planning, sittin doon there,
Cameron 'n' Clegg, oh whit a pair,
Sippin Earl Grey 'n' munchin caviar.

Double dip recession fur youse means not a jot.
Hit them wi' the bedroom tax
Benefit payments, cut the lot.
Don't have a clue how oor half live.
Take. Take. Take 'n' never give.

Sick o' hearing green shoots, economic growth, 'n' lies.
Employment's forever oan the rise.
So are prison numbers
Along wi' depression
Cos aw we get instead o' a job's a character assassination.

Ye could live on wi' us scroungers, do ye say?
Aye, maybe fur a week.
I doubt ye'd last five minutes in Farmfoods
Before some no-good scrounger broke yer beak.

Chancellor of Exchequer to Minister of the Crown.
Mastermind yer manifesto knowing fine well you let us down.
We've had weapons of mass destruction,
Expenses scandals as well.
Like yer manifestos, the truth ye'll never tell.
Bedroom tax, benefits cuts,
Why don't yis just burn us aw in hell?

Independence for Scotland or part of the UK,
Aw we want's a joab
That gies us a decent pay.

So, Government 'n' politicians
Stoap plying us wi' yer bullshit
'N' get us oot this powder keg.
Dae we really want wir weans searching for veins in their leg?
We wurny aw born wi' silver spoons like youse, Cameron and
Clegg.

PAUL

Extract from Love & Liberty
(AKA The Jolly Beggars)

See the smoking bowl before us,
  Mark our jovial ragged ring!
Round and round take up the Chorus,
  And in raptures let us sing –

A fig for those by LAW protected!
  LIBERTY's a glorious feast!
Courts for Cowards were erected,
  Churches built to please the PRIEST.

What is TITLE, what is TREASURE,
  What is REPUTATION's care?
If we lead a life of pleasure,
  'Tis no matter HOW or WHERE!

With the ready trick and fable
  Round we wander all the day;
And at night, in barn or stable,
  Hug our doxies on the hay.

Does the train-attended CARRIAGE
  Thro' the country lighter rove?
Does the sober bed of MARRIAGE
  Witness brighter scenes of love?

Life is all a VARIORUM,
  We regard not how it goes;
Let them cant about DECORUM,
  Who have character to lose.

Here's to BUDGETS, BAGS and WALLETS!
  Here's to all the wandering train!
Here's our ragged BRATS and CALLETS!
  One and all cry out, AMEN!

  A fig for those by LAW protected!
    LIBERTY'S a glorious feast!
  COURTS for Cowards were erected,
    CHURCHES built to please the priest.

ROBERT BURNS

He, rising, rejoicing,
  Between his twa Deborahs,
Looks round him an' found them
  Impatient for the Chorus.

Air — Tune, Jolly Mortals fill your glasses

See the smoking bowl before us,
  Mark our jovial, ragged ring!
Round and round take up the Chorus,
  And in raptures let us sing —
      Chorus —
    A fig for those by law protected!
    Liberty's a glorious feast!
    Courts for cowards were erected,
    Churches built to please the Priest.

What is title, what is treasure,
  What is reputation's care?
If we lead a life of pleasure,
  'Tis no matter how or where.
      A fig &c.

With the ready trick and fable
  Round we wander all the day;
And at night in barn or stable,
  Hug our doxies on the hay.
      A fig for &c.

Manuscript, *Love and Liberty – A Cantata*
Robert Burns Birthplace Museum 3.6233

INDEPENDENT MINDS

65

Outside Time

It's hell living outside time.
Stuck in limbo, doing time.
Measuring your life wasting away,
In scabby chinese chicken curries.

Passing through each pointless week,
In days of futile repetition.
We're the Fraternity of the Fallen,
Disciplined and trained for blind obedience.

The guards take pleasure as they chastise,
Part of your punishment, in their eyes.
Join the toothless snaking line,
Queue for Meth's comatose oblivion.

We're society's guilty secret,
Unseen like mushrooms in the dark.
Confined like products in a warehouse,
A state sponsored slave plantation.

Vengeance and incarceration.
Punishment and retribution.
Did I not offend enough.
To be considered with compassion.

STEPHEN

Pylons

Like Titans stretching gracefully to the skies,
their feet, to the ground, are firmly rooted.
With arms akimbo bearing their load,
their slow, solemn, snaking march continues unabated.
Selflessly delivering light and warmth across the land.
Their abrasive appearance is oft debated.
Maybe one day they'll take umbrage, walk away.
Then where will we be?

STEVEN

Slavery

Betrayed by their own kind.
Rounded up and sold for beads.
Transported across the northern sea.
Their homeland never again to see.
Encouraged to live and bred like cattle.
Their offspring born as their owners' chattel.
Sick on the boat, while shipping over.
Take them to the deck and throw them over.

Exploited by the merchant class.
Toiling daily in coal and flax.
No need for overseers here.
Whole families are queuing to volunteer.
Paid in tokens to keep them tied.
Redeemable only in the factory store.
Sick at the loom, can't work anymore.
Show them the door, there's plenty more.

Abolish slavery and free all men.
That was the claim, what was the plan.
Pay them enough for subsistence.
Use benefits to top up to existence.
Let them buy their rented houses.
Lets convert them all to debt slaves.
Sick in the call centre, ill at the bank.
Throw them on the dole, it takes up the slack.

The Asian Tiger satisfies
The western world's desire
For the latest i-devices
At the lowest unit prices.
Workers imprisoned in a factory
Miles removed from their family.
Can't stand this hell any more?
Jump from the roof to the ground below.

STEPHEN

The Tree Of Liberty

Heard ye o' the tree o' France,
  I watna what's the name o't;
Around it a' the patriots dance,
  Weel Europe kens the fame o't.
It stands where ance the Bastile stood,
  A prison built by kings, man,
When Superstition's hellish brood
  Kept France in leading-strings, man.

Upo' this tree there grows sic fruit,
  Its virtues a' can tell, man;
It raises man aboon the brute,
  It maks him ken himsel, man.
Gif ance the peasant taste a bit,
  He's greater than a lord, man,
And wi' the beggar shares a mite
  O' a' he can afford, man.

This fruit is worth a' Afric's wealth,
  To comfort us 'twas sent, man:
To gie the sweetest blush o' health,
  And mak us a' content, man
It clears the een, it cheers the heart,
  Maks high and low guid friends, man;
And he wha acts the traitor's part,
  It to perdition sends, man.

My blessings aye attend the chiel,
  Wha pitied Gallia's slaves, man,
And staw a branch, spite o' the deil,
  Frae yont the western waves, man.
Fair Virtue watered it wi' care,
  And now she sees wi' pride, man,
How weel it buds and blossoms there,
  Its branches spreading wide, man.

But vicious folk aye hate to see
  The works o' Virtue thrive, man;
The courtly vermin's banned the tree,
  And grat to see it thrive, man;
King Loui' thought to cut it down,
  When it was unco sma', man;
For this the watchman cracked his crown,
  Cut aff his head and a', man.

A wicked crew syne, on a time,
  Did tak a solemn aith, man,
It ne'er should flourish to its prime,
  I wat they pledged their faith, man.
Awa they gaed wi' mock parade,
  Like beagles hunting game, man,
But soon grew weary o' the trade,
  And wished they'd been at hame, man.

For Freedom, standing by the tree,
  Her sons did loudly ca', man;
She sang a sang o' liberty,
  Which pleased them ane and a', man
By her inspired, the new-born race
  Soon drew the avenging steel, man;
The hirelings ran-her foes gied chase,
  And banged the despot weel, man

Let Britain boast her hardy oak,
  Her poplar and her pine, man,
Auld Britain ance could crack her joke,
  And o'er her neighbours shine, man.
But seek the forest round and round,
  And soon 'twill be agreed, man,
That sic a tree can not be found
  'Twixt London and the Tweed, man.

Without this tree, alake this life
  Is but a vale o' wo, man;
A scene o' sorrow mixed wi' strife,
  Nae real joys we know, man.
We labour soon, we labour late,
  To feed the titled knave, man;
And a' the comfort we're to get,
  Is that ayont the grave, man.

Wi' plenty o' sic trees, I trow,
  The warld would live in peace, man;
The sword would help to mak a plough,
  The din o' war wad cease, man.
Like brethren in a common cause,
  We'd on each other smile, man;
And equal rights and equal laws
  Wad gladden every isle, man.

Wae worth the loon wha wadna eat
  Sic halesome dainty cheer, man;
I'd gie my shoon frae aff my feet,
  To taste sic fruit, I swear, man.
Syne let us pray, auld England may
  Sure plant this far-famed tree, man;
And blithe we'll sing, and hail the day
  That gave us liberty, man.

ROBERT BURNS

leave to say, that he has not written this last
work in his usual happy manner. — Entre nous
you know my politics; & I cannot approve of the
honest Doctor's whining over the deserved fate of a cer-
tain pair of Personages. — What is there in the delivering
over a perjured Blockhead & an unprincipled Prostitute
into the hands of the hangman, that it should arrest for
a moment, attention in an eventful hour, when
my friend Roscoe in Liverpool gloriously expresses
it — "When the welfare of Millions is hung in the one
          And the balance yet trembles with fate!"
But our friend is already indebted to people in power,
& still looks forward for his family, so I can apologize
for him, for at bottom I am sure he is a staunch
friend to liberty] — Thank God, these London trials
have given us a little more breath, & I imagine that
the time is not far distant when a man may
freely blame Billy Pit, without being called an
enemy to his Country.
                    adieu!   R Burns

Letter from Burns to Frances Wallace Dunlop
Robert Burns Birthplace Museum 3.6358

An Ode Tae Freedom

Whit's the meanin' o' this freedom?
Is it set in the Stone of Scone?
Though the English say it's treason,
      Gie a reason,
A reason why it's naw freedom.
      GI'ES A REASON.

VICTOR

Doon The Glen Burn

Doon the glen burn, we would aw run,
Screamin oot where's the bleedin sun,
But at least we were aw huvin fun,
Doon the glen burn.
Sittin starin intae the burn, it's feckin fun.

VICTOR

Independence

Who's the slave, me or you?
Is there one or more than two?
This question is asked to all of us,
And your answer is a MUST.
Throw off the yolk of Tyranny.
Let's rebuild the Scottish army.
Stand up. Shout out. SHOUT OUT.
A slave to England I'll be no more
Bring INDEPENDENCE to the fore.

VICTOR

Humanity? Yeah, Right

Death, destruction, the roar of construction,
The end, the beginning. Is it all about winning?
Children screaming, are we just dreaming?
Oil and blood it's all lost in the mud.
Americans dreaming as kids are screaming,
Dreaming of dollars as you're sitting in cellars.
Your father is dying as your mother lies crying
And all for the oil that's under your soil.
Justify your war-cry.
Drop your bombs from the sky.
Using your drones to smash their bones.
Will you sleep tight as they feel the bite?
The bite of hunger, pain and destruction.
As you scaremonger, they die of hunger.
Oh ye proud nation of the honest and caring,
Let the less human among us die without caring.
Think of them dying for your happiness.
Ask of yourself, who's the less human.

VICTOR

A Man's A Man

Is there, at honest Poverty
  That hings his head, & a' that?
The coward slave-we pass him by,
  We dare be poor for a' that!
For a' that, & a' that.
  Our toils obscure & a' that,
The rank is but the guinea's stamp,
  The Man's the gowd for a' that. –

What tho' on hamely fare we dine,
  Wear hoddin grey, & a that;
Gie fools their silks, & knaves their wine,
  A Man's a Man for a' that. –
For a' that, and a' that,
  Their tinsel show, & a' that;
The honest man, tho' e'er sae poor,
  Is king o' men for a' that. –

Ye see yon birkie ca'd, a Lord,
  Wha struts, & stares, & a' that;
Tho' hundreds worship at his word,
  He's but a coof for a' that. –
For a' that, & a' that,
  His ribband, star, & a' that;
The man of independant mind
  He looks & laughs at a' that. –

A prince can mak a belted knight,
  A marquis, duke, & a' that,
But an honest man's abon his might,
  Gude faith, he mauna fa' that!
For a' that, & a' that,
  Their dignities & a' that;
The pith o' Sense, & pride o' Worth,
  Are higher rank for a' that. –

Then let us pray, that come it may,
  As come it will for a' that,
That Sense & Worth, o'er a' the earth,
  May bear the gree, & a' that.
For a' that, & a' that,
  It's coming yet for a' that,
That Man to Man, the warld o'er,
  Shall brothers be for a' that. –

RABBIE

Some other books published by **LUATH** PRESS

Poems, Chiefly in the Scottish Dialect: The Luath Kilmarnock Edition

Robert Burns
With contributions from John Cairney and Clarke McGinn, illustrated by Bob Dewar
ISBN 978-1-906817-08-4 HBK £40

Poems, Chiefly in the Scottish Dialect, was the first collection of poetry produced by Robert Burns. Published in Kilmarnock in July 1786, it contains some of his best known poems including 'The Cotter's Saturday Night', 'To a Mouse', 'The Twa Dogs' and 'To a Mountain Daisy'. *The Luath Kilmarnock Edition* brings this classic of Scottish literature back into print.

New material includes an introduction by the 'Man Who Played Burns' – author, actor and Burns expert John Cairney – exploring Burns' life and work, especially the origins of the *Kilmarnock Edition*. Looking to the future of Burns in Scotland and the rest of the world, Clark McGinn, world-renowned Burns Supper speaker, provides an afterword that speaks to Burns' continuing legacy.

The Luath Burns Companion

John Cairney
ISBN 978-1-906817-85-5 PBK £9.99

Robert Burns was born in a thunderstorm and lived his brief life by flashes of lightning.
JOHN CAIRNEY

The collection includes 60 poems, songs and other works; and an essay that explores Burns' life and influences, his triumphs and tragedies. This informed introduction provides an insight into Burns' world.

This is not another 'complete works' but a personal selection from 'The Man Who Played Robert Burns' – John Cairney. His favourites are reproduced here and he talks about them with an obvious love of the man and his work. His depth of knowledge and understanding has been garnered over 40 years of study, writing and performance.

Burns' work has drama, passion, pathos and humour. His careful workmanship is concealed by the spontaneity of his verse. He was always a forward thinking man and remains a writer for the future.

Accent o the Mind

Rab Wilson

ISBN 978-1-905222-32-2 PBK £8.99

The 'Mither o aa Pairlaments'? A sham! They've ne'er jaloused in mair's fowr hunner years, Whit maitters maist is whit's atween yer ears!

The joy, the pain, the fear, the anger and the shame – topical and contemporary, and mostly in vibrant Scots, this is Scottish poetry at its best. Encompassing history, text messaging, politics, asylum-seeking hedgehogs and Buckfast, Rab Wilson covers the variety of modern Scottish life through refreshingly honest and often humorous poetry.

This inspirational new collection consolidates Rab Wilson's position as one of Scotland's leading poets and plays a part in the reinvigoration of the Scots language in modern Scottish society.

Bursting with ambition, technically brilliant and funny
SCOTLAND ON SUNDAY

A Map for the Blind: Poems chiefly in the Scots language

Rab Wilson

ISBN 978-1-906817-82-4 £8.99 PBK

When ah saw the wark o this lassie, wha wis developin a software programme fir fowk wi a visual impairment, the penny suddenly drapt; that poems kindae duin the same joab – they mak a pynt or reveal tae us a truth that aiblins we cuidnae see afore. An thon's the magic thing that poetry dis!
RAB WILSON

Written mostly in Scots, Rab Wilson's *A Map for the Blind* deals with topics ranging from satirical social commentary to sublime shots of everyday life with his characteristic wit and insight. From a poignant reflection into the 'black hairt' of the coal industry, to a nostalgic and spirited look at classic bicycles, to wondering if anyone was listening to 'Holy Gordon's Prayer', Rab Wilson delivers a vibrant picture of Scotland which we can't fail to recognise.

(Un)comfortably Numb: A Prison Requiem

Maureen Maguire

ISBN: 978-1-842820-01-8 PBK £8.99

Told in documentary form, this is the story of the tragedy of Yvonne Gilmour's death in Cornton Vale prison. Yvonne was one of eight inmates to take their own lives in a short period of time at the prison and her story is representative of many women in prison today.

There has been a steady increase in women prisoners since 1991, most of these women are not criminals (only one per cent are convicted for violent crimes) and two-thirds are between the ages of 15 and 30. Yvonne was one of these vulnerable young women.

The book asks relevant questions about the nature of society and shows that an alternative to prison is needed for vulnerable girls.

This is a powerful and moving indictment of 21st century Britain, told in the real voices of women behind bars, by a solicitor and teacher of many years of experience.

But N Ben A-Go-Go

Matthew Fitt

ISBN: 978-1-905222-04-9 PBK £7.99

With strong characters and a gripping plot, the well-defined settings create an atmosphere of paranoia and danger. The exciting denouement has a surprising twist and is set on Schiehallion. The introduction includes a section on how to read the Scots in this book, Mathew has made the spelling as straightforward as possible for a population used to English spelling conventions.

While But N Ben A-Go-Go *does have comic moments, the novel is far from a joke... confronting relevant issues such as global warming, epidemics and social division.*
SUNDAY HERALD

As Others See Us:
Personal views on the life
and works of Robert Burns

Portraits by Tricia Malley and Ross
Gillespie
ISBN 978 1906817 06 0 HBK £9.99
ISBN 978 1906817 52 7 PBK £7.99

As Others See Us is a unique, innovative photographic project produced by award-winning photographers Tricia Malley and Ross Gillespie

The challenge here was to capture not only each individual sitter's character but also try to convey something of the essence of his or her favourite Burns poem in a single portrait. The work of Robert Burns can be quite abstract or highly visual... sometimes both. Inspiration came from being reminded of the works of Burns, being introduced to new pieces and seeing them through the eyes of the sitters.

As we discovered during the time spent on this project, Robert Burns is just as relevant, entertaining and inspiring today as he was 250 years ago.
TRICIA MALLEY & ROSS GILLESPIE

On The Trail of Robert Burns

John Cairney
ISBN: 978-0-946487-51-6 PBK £7.99

Is there anything new to say about Robert Burns? John Cairney says it's time to trash Burns the Brand and come on the trail of the real Robert Burns. He is the best of travelling companions on this entertaining journey to the heart of the Burns story. Internationally known as 'the face of Robert Burns', John Cairney believes that the traditional Burns tourist trail urgently needs to find a new direction. In an acting career spanning forty years he has often lived and breathed Robert burns on stage. *On the Trail of Robert Burns* shows just how well he has got under the skin of Burn's complex character. This fascinating journey around Scotland is a rediscovery of Scotland's national bard as a flesh and blood genius.

Details of this and other books published by Luath Press can be found at:
www.luath.co.uk

Luath Press Limited
committed to publishing well written books worth reading

LUATH PRESS takes its name from Robert Burns, whose little collie Luath (*Gael.,* swift or nimble) tripped up Jean Armour at a wedding and gave him the chance to speak to the woman who was to be his wife and the abiding love of his life. Burns called one of 'The Twa Dogs' Luath after Cuchullin's hunting dog in Ossian's *Fingal*. Luath Press was established in 1981 in the heart of Burns country, and now resides a few steps up the road from Burns' first lodgings on Edinburgh's Royal Mile.

Luath offers you distinctive writing with a hint of unexpected pleasures.

Most bookshops in the UK, the US, Canada, Australia, New Zealand and parts of Europe either carry our books in stock or can order them for you. To order direct from us, please send a £sterling cheque, postal order, international money order or your credit card details (number, address of cardholder and expiry date) to us at the address below. Please add post and packing as follows: UK – £1.00 per delivery address; overseas surface mail – £2.50 per delivery address; overseas airmail – £3.50 for the first book to each delivery address, plus £1.00 for each additional book by airmail to the same address. If your order is a gift, we will happily enclose your card or message at no extra charge.

Luath Press Limited
543/2 Castlehill
The Royal Mile
Edinburgh EH1 2ND
Scotland
Telephone: 0131 225 4326 (24 hours)
Fax: 0131 225 4324
email: sales@luath.co.uk
Website: www.luath.co.uk